Boom Boom Pirates

Maverick
Early Readers

'Boom Boom Pirates'
An original concept by Amanda Brandon
© Amanda Brandon 2021

Illustrated by Tanja Varcelija

Published by MAVERICK ARTS PUBLISHING LTD

Studio 11, City Business Centre, 6 Brighton Road,

Horsham, West Sussex, RH13 5BB

© Maverick Arts Publishing Limited November 2021

+44 (0)1403 256941

A CIP catalogue record for this book is available at the British Library.

ISBN 978-1-84886-829-8

www.maverickbooks.co.uk

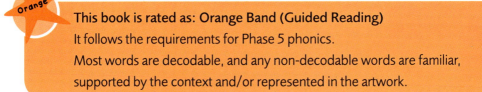

Orange

This book is rated as: Orange Band (Guided Reading)
It follows the requirements for Phase 5 phonics.
Most words are decodable, and any non-decodable words are familiar,
supported by the context and/or represented in the artwork.

Boom Boom
Pirates

by
Amanda Brandon

illustrated by
Tanja Varcelija

Captain Tiptoe could not sleep.

His crew were too noisy.

Boom! Boom! The pirates played skittles with cannon balls and bottles.

"Go to bed," Captain Tiptoe shouted.

He put his fingers in his ears.

But the pirates did not go to bed.

Biff! Bash! They had a pillow fight.

Feathers flew everywhere.

"Shivering sharks!" A pillow whizzed

over the captain's head.

He rushed back to bed and put on
some earmuffs.

Bang! Bang! The pirates took out their tools and hammered planks on the deck.

"OUCH! Stinky seaweed!" Captain Tiptoe tripped on a plank. He hopped back to bed.

He put his earmuffs on tight and pulled the blanket over his head. "What can I do?" Captain Tiptoe said.

"I must stop the pirates making

so much noise at night!"

Suddenly, he had a good idea.

At bedtime the next night, Captain Tiptoe gave the pirates a map. It had a big X on it.

"Yippee! A treasure hunt!" they said.

Captain Tiptoe had also put an X on each pirate's hammock. The pirates rushed to find the Xs.

Under each pillow they found a cuddly teddy.

Soon all the pirates were tucked in their hammocks. Captain Tiptoe fetched his big book of Treasure Tales and told them a story.

"One day a pirate ship landed on a secret beach. The pirates found golden coins and sparkly gems..."

"Lovely..." Cabin Boy hugged his teddy.

"Super..." Cook snuggled in his pyjamas.

"Mmmm..." First Mate pulled the covers up.

Captain Tiptoe blew out the lights.

"Sweet dreams. Sleep tight.

Don't let the bed bugs bite.

Work and play in the day is best.

At night it's time to rest."

Waves rocked the ship gently.

The pirates nodded off under the bright

moon. They dreamed of maps and gold coins.

Captain Tiptoe closed his book

and sighed happily.

"Hurrah! Now I don't need these."

He tossed away his earmuffs and he slept and slept until...

...his parrot began to SQUAWK!

Quiz

1. Why couldn't Captain Tiptoe sleep?
a) His bed was too creaky
b) His tummy was to rumbly
c) His crew were too noisy

2. What did the map have on it?
a) A big X
b) A small parrot
c) A big circle

3. What did the pirates find under their pillows?
a) A blanket
b) Earmuffs
c) A cuddly teddy

4. What book did Captain Tiptoe read?
a) Treasure Tales
b) Sea Adventures
c) Pirates Ahoy

5. What sound does the parrot make?
a) EEK!
b) SQUAWK!
c) HELLO!

Turn over for answers

Book Bands for Guided Reading

Pink
Red
Yellow
Blue
Green
Orange
Turquoise
Purple
Gold
White

The Institute of Education book banding system is a scale of colours that reflects the various levels of reading difficulty. The bands are assigned by taking into account the content, the language style, the layout and phonics. Word, phrase and sentence level work is also taken into consideration.

Maverick Early Readers are a bright, attractive range of books covering the pink to white bands. All of these books have been book banded for guided reading to the industry standard and edited by a leading educational consultant.

To view the whole Maverick Readers scheme, visit our website at

www.maverickearlyreaders.com

Or scan the QR code above to view our scheme instantly!

Quiz Answers: 1c, 2a, 3c, 4a, 5b